ANSWERS
4 LIFE

ANSWERS
4 LIFE

From CHAOS *to* CALM
in **35 days**

DERVON DUNAGAN

XULON PRESS

Xulon Press
2301 Lucien Way #415
Maitland, FL 32751
407.339.4217
www.xulonpress.com

Printed in the United States of America.

ISBN-13: 978-1-6628-1253-8
Hardcover ISBN-13: 978-1-6628-1254-5
Ebook: ISBN-13: 978-1-6628-1255-2

TABLE OF CONTENTS

INTRODUCTION

MY STORY- THE EYES HAVE IT

During my early adult years, I really enjoyed going to the movie theatre. I'd salivate over movies such as "Halloween," "Friday the 13th," "Scarface," and "Wall Street." What I did not understand at the time that those movies slowly had a profound effect on my thinking and my perspective on life. They filled my mind with a dark perspective that affected everything I did in my life.

> - Matthew 6:23 (NLT) But when your eye is bad, your whole body is filled with darkness. And if the light you think you have is actually darkness, how deep that darkness is!

> I didn't have a clue about temptation; I acted on my desires... lust of the flesh, and lust of the eyes!!

> - James 1:14-15 (NLT)

> 14- Temptation comes from our own desires, which entice us and drag us away.

> 15–These desires give birth to sinful actions. And when sin is allowed to grow, it gives birth to death.

There's a progression in Our vision, our desires which determines if our eyes bring in light (goodness) to our bodies (our being / soul) Or Darkness (things NOT pleasing to Jesus–selfish ambitions)

The progression of our eyes begins with a GLANCE, then a LOOK, then a GAZE ... DESIRE

Our eyes are either good or they are bad.

The brain is a mighty organ that transmits / delivers impulses-messages (information) to every part of our bodies creating movements.

The brain stores information, processes it, transforming it into knowledge.

Behind your brain (physical brain) is your MIND––the spiritual brain–– your conscience. Your MIND(spiritual brain) reasons the right things to do (righteous living) and it reasons the WRONG things to do (sinful).

The heart–we obviously have a physical heart which is the centrality of life; your heart pumps blood (in the blood is life) through your arteries to every part of your body.

The life in your blood which travels through your arteries, Delivers life to all of your components.

Behind your physical heart is your spiritual heart.

Your spiritual heart receives information from your brain , then to your MIND, then to your spiritual heart.

This information is then converted into your UNDERSTANDING ; this is NOT knowledge!–- knowledge is information stored in your physical brain.

UNDERSTANDING is from your spiritual heart which is how a person REASONS their way of life; how you operate.

- Psalm 119:34 (NLT)

Give me understanding and I will obey your instructions; I will put them into practice with all my heart.

- Philippians 1:9 (NLT)

I pray that your love will overflow more and more, and that you will keep on growing in knowledge and understanding.

-Psalm 119:104 (NLT)

Your commandments give me understanding; no wonder I hate every false way of life.

Eyes--your physical eyes receives images that are sent to your brain, leaving a permanent impression.

Behind your physical eyes are your spiritual eyes.

The spiritual eyes are connected to your MIND (spiritual brain), then to your spiritual heart.

- Proverbs 23:26 (NLT)

O my son, give me your heart. May your eyes take delight in following my ways.

- Proverbs 21:4 (NLT)

Haughty eyes, a proud heart, and evil actions are all sin.

In those days, (my 20's and 30's) when I believed I was doing a good deed for someone—–financially or any other assistance (light , goodness)—– my motives were WRONG. It wasn't from the treasury of a good heart...

After helping someone (good deed ,) I'd think to myself : " I helped them, so they'd BETTER help me if I need it "

My so-called "good deed"(light) was for self-gratification and future return on investment.

The light wasn't truly light at all. It was really darkness!!

> - Matthew 6:22-23 (NLT) 22–"Your eye is a lamp that provides light for your body. When your eye is good, your whole body is filled with light.
>
> 23- But when your eye is bad, your whole body is filled with darkness. And if the light you think you have is actually darkness, how deep that darkness is!

Watching a fist fight right in front of me(in real life) was INTERESTING to me, and I considered it to be a GOOD FIGHT if someone suffered injury.

Thinking back on those days, I presently cry out within my heart--" WHAT A WRETCH!!"

Yes, my eyes were bad.

So, what's having a good eye?

How does a good eye bring light to your whole body?

> - Joshua 1:8 (NLT) Study this Book of Instruction continually. Meditate on it day and night so you will be sure to obey everything written in it. Only then will you prosper and succeed in all you do.

- Matthew 22:37-39 (NLT) 37 -Jesus replied, "'You must love the LORD your God with all your heart, all your soul, and all your mind.'

- 38 This is the first and greatest commandment.

-39 A second is equally important: 'Love your neighbor as yourself.'

- Luke 6:33-34 (NLT)

33–And if you do good only to those who do good to you, why should you get credit? Even sinners do that much!

-34 And if you lend money only to those who can repay you, why should you get credit? Even sinners will lend to other sinners for a full return.

- Luke 11:36 (NLT) If you are filled with light, with no dark corners, then your whole life will be radiant, as though a floodlight were filling you with light."

Always be eager to help others; you will experience a JOY that will flood your heart when Jesus is the center of your life.

This joy is NOT self-gratification!- -

Choosing Jesus as the LORD of my life, is the best decision I ever made.

I still have far to go, but my faith is in Him alone and JESUS is the ULTIMATE OPTHAMOLOGIST. Jesus is constantly improving my vision (spiritual eyes),and at some point, my vision will improve from 20/20 VISION–to heavenly/kingdom vision

My prayer for you as you read and process the questions posed in this "THIRTY- FIVE **Day Study: Chaos to Calm"** is from Philippians 1:9 which says, *"I pray that your love will overflow more and more, and that **you will keep on growing in knowledge and understanding**"* (NLT emphasis added).

Week 1

What Happens After You Die?

I HAVE A QUESTION THAT REQUIRES **SERIOUS THOUGHT;**
IF SOMETHING **TRAGIC** WERE TO HAPPEN TO YOU TODAY
AND YOU LEAVE THIS **EARTH-- WHERE WILL YOU SPEND
ETERNITY? HEAVEN** (ETERNAL LIFE)? OR **HELL**(ETERNAL
PUNISHMENT)?

(1) TOMORROW IS NOT PROMISED

(2) THE NEXT HOUR OF YOUR LIFE IS NOT GUARANTEED

(3) THE NEXT **10** MINUTES MAY NEVER ARRIVE. **MEDITATE ON
IT. HEAVEN** IS **REAL,HELL** IS **REAL, ETERNITY** IS **REAL.**

HERE ARE **8** FREQUENTED COMMENTS REGARDING GOD, HELL,
SATAN/DEVIL FOLLOWED BY ANSWERS:

(1) " SATAN/THE DEVIL **ISN'T** REAL"

ANSWER–**1** PETER **5:8 (NLT)** STAY ALERT! WATCH
OUT FOR YOUR GREAT ENEMY, THE DEVIL. HE
PROWLS AROUND LIKE A ROARING LION, LOOKING
FOR SOMEONE TO DEVOUR.

1

(2) "THERE'S NO GOD!"

> ANSWER–PSALMS 53:1 (NLT) ONLY FOOLS SAY IN THEIR HEARTS, "THERE IS NO GOD." THEY ARE CORRUPT, AND THEIR ACTIONS ARE EVIL; NOT ONE OF THEM DOES GOOD!

(3) "I'M NOT A SINNER!"

> ANSWER–ROMANS 3:23 (NLT) FOR EVERYONE HAS SINNED; WE ALL FALL SHORT OF GOD'S GLORIOUS STANDARD.

(4) "I SHOULDN'T GO TO HELL BECAUSE I AM A GOOD PERSON"

> ANSWER- ROMANS 3:12 (NLT) ALL HAVE TURNED AWAY; ALL HAVE BECOME USELESS. NO ONE DOES GOOD, NOT A SINGLE ONE."

(5) "I DO A LOT OF NICE THINGS FOR PEOPLE"

ANSWER- WITHOUT ACCEPTING JESUS AS "YOUR" LORD AND SAVIOR:

> - ISAIAH 64:6 (NLT) WE ARE ALL INFECTED AND IMPURE WITH SIN. WHEN WE DISPLAY OUR RIGHTEOUS DEEDS, THEY ARE NOTHING BUT FILTHY RAGS. LIKE AUTUMN LEAVES, WE WITHER AND FALL, AND OUR SINS SWEEP US AWAY LIKE THE WIND.

(6) "WHEN I DIE I WON'T FEEL ANYTHING"

ANSWER- **WRONG!!**

- LUKE 16:23-24 (NLT) 23 AND HIS SOUL WENT TO THE PLACE OF THE DEAD. THERE, IN TORMENT, HE SAW ABRAHAM IN THE FAR DISTANCE WITH LAZARUS AT HIS SIDE.

- 24 "THE RICH MAN SHOUTED, 'FATHER ABRAHAM, HAVE SOME PITY! SEND LAZARUS OVER HERE TO DIP THE TIP OF HIS FINGER IN WATER AND COOL MY TONGUE. I AM IN ANGUISH IN THESE FLAMES.'

(7) "I'M LOOKING FORWARD TO GOING TO HELL, I GET TO SEE ALL OF MY FRIENDS"

ANSWER–**WRONG!** YOU WON'T SEE ANYTHING!!

- 2 PETER 2:4 (NLT) FOR GOD DID NOT SPARE EVEN THE ANGELS WHO SINNED. HE THREW THEM INTO HELL, IN GLOOMY PITS OF DARKNESS, WHERE THEY ARE BEING HELD UNTIL THE DAY OF JUDGMENT.

(8) " I CAN'T WAIT TO GET TO HELL, IT'S GOING TO BE ONE BIG PARTY"

ANSWER- **WRONG!!** -MATTHEW 13:42 (NLT) AND THE ANGELS WILL THROW THEM INTO THE

FIERY FURNACE, WHERE THERE WILL BE WEEPING
AND GNASHING OF TEETH.

FRIENDS, HELL IS REAL; ONCE YOU CLOSE YOUR EYES FOR THE
LAST TIME HERE ON EARTH, YOU WILL OPEN THEM IN THE PRESENCE
OF THE LORD AND EVERY BELIEVER OF THE "LORD", WHO HAS
EVER LIVED ON EARTH OR OPEN YOUR EYES IN HELL.

- LUKE 16:22-23 (NLT) 22 "FINALLY, THE POOR
MAN DIED AND WAS CARRIED BY THE ANGELS TO BE
WITH ABRAHAM. THE RICH MAN ALSO DIED AND WAS
BURIED,–23 AND HIS SOUL WENT TO THE PLACE OF
THE DEAD. THERE, IN TORMENT, HE SAW ABRAHAM
IN THE FAR DISTANCE WITH LAZARUS AT HIS SIDE.

SOME MAY SAY–"I DON'T CARE WHAT THE BIBLE SAYS, I STILL
DON'T BELIEVE THERE'S A HELL. WHEN I DIE, I WON'T KNOW IT AND
I'LL JUST CEASE TO EXIST."

OKAY, FOR THE SAKE OF CONVERSATION, LET'S SAY YOU ARE
RIGHT(YOU'RE NOT! , THIS IS ONLY FOR CONVERSATION)--
EVERYONE DIES, AND IT'S OVER–I SAY GREAT

BUT WHAT IF YOU'RE WRONG?-----THERE ARE NO
SECOND CHANCES.

THIS IS YOUR ONLY CHANCE IN THIS LIFE TO BE SAVED.

TOMORROW, THE NEXT HOUR ,THE NEXT 10 MINUTES MAY
NEVER ARRIVE.

WHERE WILL YOU GO? HEAVEN OR HELL

THINK ABOUT IT!!

REFLECTION

DAY 1
WHERE WILL YOU
SPEND ETERNITY?

- Matthew 25:41 (NLT) "Then the King will turn to those on the left and say, 'Away with you, you cursed ones, into the eternal fire prepared for the devil and his demons.

- Matthew 25:46 (NLT) "And they will go away into eternal punishment, but the righteous will go into eternal life."

There is a hell, but hell was prepared for the devil and his demons, NOT for people, but people send themselves to hell. After hell comes the lake of fire.

WHY?

Because of their unbelief and rejection of JESUS as the LORD and SAVIOR of their lives; thus a lifestyle of evil deeds(all things not pleasing to God-- wrong doings).

Think of it this way, our prisons/jails are made for those who break the laws that govern the land. The innocent and law abiding citizens will never see a prison because prison/jail is ONLY to house wrong-doers.

Hell is the same way; those who do not accept JESUS, who took ALL OF OUR WRONG/ WICKED DEEDS upon HIMSELF ON THE CROSS, paid the penalty that we all deserve, so we can go free (to Heaven with Jesus forever) and NOT to JAIL/HELL.

REFLECTION

DAY 2
ETERNITY: HEAVEN OR HELL?

M atthew 13:49-50 (NLT) 49 That is the way it will be at the end of the world. The angels will come and separate the wicked people from the righteous,–50 Throwing the wicked into the fiery furnace, where there will be weeping and gnashing of teeth.

The world is coming to an end, and when the nonbeliever take their last breath here on earth, their next breath will be standing before ALMIGHTY GOD, to receive judgment for not accepting Jesus into their hearts as their Lord and savior and for every wrong deed committed throughout their lives.

Hell and then the fiery furnace (lake of fire) is their destination- forever.

Hell is an extremely uncomfortable place; so excruciating, that those who didn't accept OUR sin bearer (JESUS) will grind their teeth day and night – non-stop for eternity.

Once judged by ALMIGHTY GOD, the angels will escort (throw) the nonbeliever to hell, fiery furnace (lake of fire), similar to a prison guard escorting a convicted felon to their jail cell to live out their prison sentence.

REFLECTION

DAY 3
ETERNITY: DARKNESS OR LIGHT?

Jude 1:13 (CEV) 13 Their shameful deeds show up like foam on wild ocean waves. They are like wandering stars forever doomed to the darkest pits of hell.

Blackest darkness is as dark as dark can get!

Hell and the lake of fire is the opposite of heaven.

WHY?

Because wherever the LORD is NOT present, there's nothing good. God/Jesus created ALL of the lights in the heavens and HE (God) is light.

Satan is the prince of darkness and there is NO light in him nor his kingdom.

Those who chose NOT to accept Jesus into their hearts, who paid the penalty for our sins, have chosen the kingdom of darkness as their eternal destination.

How dark is that darkness?

And what does that darkness symbolize?

A terrifyingly thick darkness; so thick you can feel it and so terrifying that you won't want to move an inch. So dark that you can't see your hand in front of your face.

This darkness symbolizes the darkness that filled the hearts and lives of those who didn't receive Jesus as their savior from eternal condemnation--- everyone who live their lives without Jesus, who is the light of the world and the light of life, is in the dark.

REFLECTION

DAY 4
ETERNITY: WILL I
REALLY SEE GOD?

- Revelation 4:2-3 (NLT) 2 And instantly I was
in the Spirit, and I saw a throne in heaven and
someone sitting on it.

- 3 The one sitting on the throne was as brilliant as
gemstones—like jasper and carnelian. And the glow
of an emerald circled his throne like a rainbow.

The Apostle John who wrote the book of Revelation, was personally summoned by Jesus in the spirit up to heaven to get a future look at the things that must take place and what heaven will look like.(Revelation 4)

The Apostle John does his very best to describe what he sees--- the glory of heaven, its opulence and most importantly the ALMIGHTY GOD sitting on His throne. Heaven is simply INDESCRIBABLE!!

REFLECTION

Day 5
Eternity: What Will I Really See?

E ternity: Heaven & the new Jerusalem

- Revelation 21:1-2 (NLT) 1 Then I saw a new heaven and a new earth, for the old heaven and the old earth had disappeared. And the sea was also gone.

- 2 And I saw the holy city, the new Jerusalem, coming down from God out of heaven like a bride beautifully dressed for her husband.

Almighty God said, "Look, I am making everything new" (Rev.21:5); this includes a new heaven and a new earth.

The sea will be gone; the sea, in antiquity, symbolized/represented CHAOS and was seen as a raging, threatening, and fearful place. The Lord often calmed the sea.

This new heaven/new Jerusalem, built by the Lord, will be BEYOND stunning and will be the abode of God/Jesus and EVERY BELIEVER to ever live.

REFLECTION

DAY 6
ETERNITY: I WANT TO SEE THE TRUE LIGHT

Revelation 21:23 (NLT) And the city has no need of sun or moon, for the glory of God illuminates the city, and the Lamb is its light.

The new heaven/new city Jerusalem will be self-sufficient because the source of ALL life and light will be there--God/Jesus (the Lamb) the true light; thus no need of the sun or moon which HE created. The old heaven and earth will have passed away.

Where there's eternal light, there's eternal life.

Day 7
Do you know where you will go when you die?

There are no second chances. This is your only chance in this life to be saved.

Will you choose Heaven or Hell?

My Journal

Write a Letter or Prayer to God telling Him if you trust or mistrust Jesus Christ as your Lord and Savior and explaining why:

_____

_____

_____

_____

_____

_____

_____

_____

ANSWERS 4 LIFE:

_____

_____

_____

_____

_____

_____

_____

_____

_____

_____

_____

_____

_____

_____

_____

_____

_____

_____

_____

WEEK 2

AM I RIGHT WITH GOD?

-Romans 3:22 (NLT) We are made right with God by placing our faith in Jesus Christ. And this is true for everyone who believes, no matter who we are.

"WELL, I'M A GOOD PERSON, I'M ALRIGHT, I DON'T NEED JESUS TO BE RIGHT WITH GOD!"

- Romans 3:10-12 (NLT) 10 As the Scriptures say, "No one is righteous— not even one.

- 11 No one is truly wise; no one is seeking God.

- 12 All have turned away; all have become useless. No one does good, not a single one."

"Well, I haven't murdered anyone, I don't steal, I'm good to my parents, I love my wife and kids, and I give to the SAVE THE WHALE FOUNDATION. I don't sin."

- Romans 3:23 (NLT) For everyone has sinned; we all fall short of God's glorious standard.

"OKAY, WHAT HAS JESUS EVER DONE FOR ME?"

- Romans 3:25 (NLT) For God presented Jesus as the sacrifice for sin. People are made right with God when they believe that Jesus sacrificed his life, shedding his blood. This sacrifice shows that God was being fair when he held back and did not punish those who sinned in times past,

"Okay, if I BELIEVE WHAT YOU ARE SAYING; then is there more I need to do?"
YES:

-Romans 10:9 (NLT) If you confess with your mouth that Jesus is Lord and believe in your heart that God raised him from the dead, you will be saved.

"IS THAT ALL?"

- Romans 10:10 (NLT) For it is by believing in your heart that you are made right with God, and it is by confessing with your mouth that you are saved.

"WHAT ABOUT MY FAMILY?"

-Romans 10:13 (NLT) For "Everyone who calls on the name of the LORD will be saved."

ETERNAL LIFE WITH THE LORD JESUS IS "YOURS" IF YOU CHOOSE.

MEDITATE

DAY 1
WHAT ABOUT MY GOOD DEEDS?

Isaiah 64:6 tells us, *"We are all infected and impure with sin. **When we display our righteous deeds, they are nothing but filthy rags.** Like autumn leaves, we wither and fall, and our sins sweep us away like the wind."* (NLT)

We are all born with a sin nature. When we perform our "good deeds" we **only** glorify ourselves, bolstering pride. The Lord hates pride (Proverbs 16:18 and 8:13). Without asking Jesus' forgiveness for our sins and accepting Him as the Lord of our lives, we remain living and spiraling deeper into sin and we are swept away.

MEDITATE

DAY 2
BUT I DON'T STEAL,
MURDER, OR CHEAT?

James 2:10-11 warns, *"For the person who keeps all of the laws except one is as guilty as a person who has broken all of God's laws. For the same God who said, 'You must not commit adultery,' also said, 'You must not murder.' So if you murder someone but do not commit adultery, you have still broken the law."* (NLT)

The person who tries to live a morally good life; basically trying to keep God's Law---the 10 commandments, is trying to do so without the spirit of God living on the inside of them-- without accepting Jesus as Lord and savior.

It's impossible for mankind to keep the Ten Commandments every day for life. We **must** keep them **all** in order to be right with God, but it's impossible. God can only be in the presence of holiness, so once we accept Jesus as Lord and Savior, who kept all the laws, God then sees us as righteous, as though He is looking at His Son.

Jesus kept the **entire** law perfectly for everyone that will believe in Him.

MEDITATE

DAY 3
AM I SEEKING GOD?

P roverbs 8:17 assures us, *"I love all who love me. Those who search will surely find me."* (NLT)

Seeking the Lord through His Word, prayer, and meditation is to have a desire, a craving to know Him, His ways, and His heart. You will develop a burning desire to understand **all** that you can about Him and be with Him; like that special person in your life. This is the same desire we are to have for Jesus. When we seek/pursue Him, we will surely find Him. When we find Him, He will reveal more and more of Himself to us. Just as in dating, the more we seek, the better we get to know the person.

MEDITATE

DAY 4
IS JESUS THE WAY?

In John 14:6, *Jesus told him, "I am the way, the truth, and the life. No one can come to the Father except through me."* (NLT)

There's **absolutely no other way** to Heaven and the Father except by way of the Lord Jesus! Jesus is the door to heaven and there's only one door. It's like you were imprisoned, and your bail was $3 billion dollars and Jesus pays it because He loves you and wants to set you free. He was the **only one** who could pay such a price for your **freedom** from **everlasting** condemnation. This freedom, our salvation, is a gift. He didn't have to do it. We can receive this wonderful free gift by accepting Jesus as our Lord and Savior. Then, we can **know** that we are right with God.

MEDITATE

DAY 5
IS MY LIFESTYLE
RIGHT WITH GOD?

1 Corinthians 6:9-11 explains, *"Don't you realize that those who do wrong will not inherit the Kingdom of God? Don't fool yourselves. Those who indulge in sexual sin, or who worship idols, or commit adultery, or are male prostitutes, or practice homosexuality, or are thieves, or greedy people, or drunkards, or are abusive, or cheat people—none of these will inherit the Kingdom of God. Some of you were once like that. But you were cleansed; you were made holy;* **you were made right with God by calling on the name of the Lord Jesus Christ and by the Spirit of our God.***"* (NLT)

This lifestyle is **not** pleasing to the Lord and separates us from God. Allowing Jesus to shape and mold our hearts, we begin to view life differently and our hope of the future grows brighter. We begin to realize and experience the wonderful plan and promises He has for our lives. The former lifestyle will no longer be desirable; it WILL change, and disappear over time. His precious blood cleanses us of that former lifestyle and we become holy in the sight of the Lord and in right standing with God.

MEDITATE

DAY 6
IS MY FAITH RIGHT WITH GOD?

Hebrews 11:6 says, *"And it is impossible to please God without faith. Anyone who wants to come to him must believe that God exists and that he rewards those who sincerely seek him."* (NLT)

What is faith?

Hebrews 11:1 explains, *"Faith is the confidence that what we hope for will actually happen; it gives us assurance about things we cannot see."* (NLT)

Have faith in Jesus because:
- He saves us from eternal fire
- He's our healer, guiding the hands of the doctor, giving wisdom and the discernment needed to make critical decisions for your care.
- He provides the air we breathe.
- He keeps us safe and out of harm's way even when we don't realize it.
- He opens doors (opportunities) that NO man can shut.

- He makes a way out of Difficult situations when There is NO way.
- He gives you answers to solve problems that you've never had prior knowledge of.
- He will have your enemies do nice things for you and they won't know why they're doing them.

Jesus can do for you what you can't do for yourself in difficult situations.

Day 7
Being right with God includes having faith in Jesus—He is the only door to heaven and a right standing with God.

- Mark 11:24 tells us, *"The Lord moves on our behalf when we pray to Him and truly believe that He will act."* (NLT)

My Journal

Write a Letter or Prayer to God asking Him what you need to do to be right with Him:

_____

_____

_____

_____

_____

_____

_____

_____

WEEK 3

ARE YOU A REFLECTION OF GOD'S CHARACTER?

As believers, OUR glory comes from the LORD JESUS. We are a reflection of HIS RADIANCE.

Have you ever been in the presence of someone and that person had a certain " GLOW" about them?

Everything about that person is bright and attractive.

Jesus (in the flesh, in human form) was/is a reflection of the FATHER'S glory and brilliance, but Jesus' radiance is veiled with skin.

If Jesus were to walk among the people in His day, in His TRUE form–His glory, His brilliance--- it would be TOO MUCH for the human eyes.

>-Matthew 17:2 (NLT) As the men watched, Jesus' appearance was transformed so that his face shone like the sun, and his clothes became as white as light.

>- Acts 9:3-5 (NIV) 3 As he neared Damascus on his journey, suddenly a light from heaven flashed around him.

- 4 He fell to the ground and heard a voice say to him, "Saul, Saul, why do you persecute me?"

- 5 "Who are you, Lord?" Saul asked. "I am Jesus, whom you are persecuting," he replied.

At birth, we (humanity) are born in darkness–inwardly (sinners). When we give our lives to CHRIST, we are indwelt with His Holy Spirit, and NOW have the light of the Lord.

in this new life with Jesus, this light is only a flicker–––the size of one small candle for a cake.

The more the believer seeks a deeper relationship with the Lord; the flickering dim candle light grows within us into a STEADY brighter light.

This light, as the believer continues to grow in Christ Jesus, begins to shine brighter and shine through our veil called skin (flesh, humanity, our being, personality, character).

Moses' relationship with God was SO close that Moses reflected the radiance of the LORD.

PONDER

Day 1
Are You a Reflection of God's Glory?

2 Corinthians(CEV) 3:18 says, *"So our faces are not covered. They show the bright glory of the Lord, as the Lord's Spirit makes us more and more like our glorious Lord"*

Jesus is glorious and His glory is brighter than the noon-day sun.

The glory of God, reflected in His Son Jesus, was His character and His goodness here on earth. His goodness is so pure and absolute that in His true form (not covered or veiled with human skin), it is so brilliant with a glorious radiance that the human eye cannot look upon His splendor.

Jesus called us out of the life of darkness (the veil) into His marvelous light and now we are children of the light.

Because the Spirit of the Lord lives in us, we share in this shining glory. The Holy Spirit guides us in living a life pleasing to the Lord. Our good deeds are the leading of the Holy Spirit. These godly deeds and godly way of life are noticed by others and are life-giving to them.

We, the believers, shine brightly to others because of the radiance within us because of the glory of the Lord within shining through.

PONDER

Day 2
Are You a Reflection of God's Radiance?

Psalm 112:4 says, *"Light shines in the darkness for the godly. They are generous, compassionate, and righteous"* (NLT).

Radiance is by definition:

1. brightness or light
2. warm,cheerful brightness.
3. brilliance, luminescence.

One who is walking (in relationship) with the Lord is being transformed by the Lord into the character of the Lord every day. God is light and light is good. Everything involving light is beneficial. Light cuts through and extinguishes darkness. His goodness is beyond great. His light is glorious and brilliant.

God's character shines in and through the believer. The attributes of the Lord increase as we continue our relationship with Jesus like:

1. Generosity- the willingness and readiness to give freely.
2. Compassion- pity, sympathy, deep concern for the sufferings or misfortunes of others.

3. Righteousness- a life of integrity, God's own perfection in every attribute, every attitude, every behavior, and every word.

This righteousness **only** comes from our relationship with Jesus. He is the only righteous one and He lives within us. Thus, we are righteous in His sight and we are a reflection of His radiance.

PONDER

DAY 3
ARE YOU A REFLECTION OF GOD'S LIGHT?

I saiah 58:10 tells us to, *"Feed the hungry, and help those in trouble. Then your light will shine out from the darkness, and the darkness around you will be as bright as noon"* (NLT).

In John 8:12, Jesus said, *"I am the light of the world..."* (NLT).

Jesus also said, ***"You are the light of the world..."*** (Matthew 5:14 NLT).

We live in a world filled with people doing deeds of darkness, but once you accept Jesus as Lord and Savior and allow Him to be the center of your life, He then takes up residency in your heart and becomes the **light** of your life.

Now you will begin to live a life of light that is life-giving to others—a life of love and goodness and generosity.

Jesus called us out of darkness to be a light to the dark unbelieving world.

We become more like Him as this light extinguishes the darkness around us. This glorious light is attractive to many and especially those in need.

PONDER

Day 4
Are You a Reflection of God's Magnificent Kingdom?

Romans 13:13 says, *"Because we belong to the day, we must live decent lives for all to see. Don't participate in the darkness of wild parties and drunkenness, or in sexual promiscuity and immoral living, or in quarreling and jealousy"* (NLT).

Night is the opposite of day. Night represents the lifestyle of darkness and the efforts to keep it hidden.

Day represents **light** and a lifestyle of right living. Everything in the light/day is exposed for all to see. The believers are children of the day.

You belong to the day!

In the life of the believer, it's paramount to live a life of **integrity, righteousness, and decency.**

Why? Because once you receive Jesus as the Lord of your life, you become a representative of His **magnificent kingdom**. Your lifestyle **must** be transparent. Over time, those deeds of darkness - lifestyle that we used to partake of, will begin to fade. Those desires will become undesirable. However, we **must** lean on the Lord Jesus to help us overcome those old desires, because in our human strength we can't conquer them apart from Him.

He will help us do it when we do our part in overcoming our old nature, so we can truly reflect God's Magnificent Kingdom of light!

PONDER

DAY 5
ARE YOU A REFLECTION OF GOD'S GLORY IN UNITY?

J ohn 17:22 says, *"I have given them the glory you gave me, so they may be **one as we are one"** (NLT).

The glory of the Lord Jesus is revealed through His character, goodness, and works. Jesus' glory was manifested in His lifestyle here on earth and His death on the cross.

The Father and the Son are **"One"** in unity. God the Son, Jesus, is the **exact** likeness of God the Father. He was the glory of the Father revealed to the world, but specifically to the disciples. His loving desire was for them to be in **oneness** (unity) with Him so they would be a reflection of the unity of the Father and Son.

God the Son, Jesus, gave His disciples this same glory so they and every believer thereafter would be one (in unity) just as the Father and Son are **One**.

The children of God express this supernatural glory of loving unity among one another (John 13:35). The children of God are one with each other and are one with Jesus and **Jesus is One with the Father**.

This **oneness** is a **loving unity** and is **radiant** and **attractive** to a dark world that cannot embrace nor grasp a loving **oneness** with others. this **only** comes from God through a relationship with Jesus. This is manifested through the believers from Lord Jesus and is glorious.

PONDER

DAY 6
ARE YOU A REFLECTION OF GOD'S ASSURANCE OF HIS PROTECTION?

P salm 3:3 says, *"But you, O LORD, are a shield around me;* **you are my glory**, *the one who holds my head high"* (NLT).

The Lord is central in the life of the believer. When the children of God place their trust in Him for **all** things, their faith and confidence will increase.

In difficult, life-threatening times, when believers are under attack, we can **know** that the Lord is our shield, our impenetrable fortress. This is not just physically, but spiritually as well.

The enemy (satan and his demons) will use many methods to knock the child of God off of the path of righteous living—fear, people to slander you, harm, discouragement, depression, and theft of your joy (John 10:10). However, we have the **assurance** that the Lord will shield us, protect us, comfort us, encourage us, and lift our heads high.

Mankind finds glory in power, material possessions, prestige, and fame, but **your glory** is found in the Lord.

The world (the non-believing world) boasts in their position, accomplishments, beauty, and wealth, but **all** good things come from the Lord, so boast in the Lord because **your glory is in the Lord**.

The people in your life—family, friends, neighbors, colleagues, etc. **all** observe your life. When you experience difficulties, your glory shines brilliantly because of the manner in which you dealt with the crisis. The Lord is glorified in this because He lives **in you** and those around you marvel at this.

DAY 7
MY JOURNAL

*W*RITE *A* L*ETTER OR* P*RAYER TO* G*OD ASKING* H*IM TO SHOW YOU HOW TO TRULY BE A REFLECTION OF* H*IS GLORY, RADIANCE, LIGHT,* H*IS MAGNIFICENT KINGDOM,* H*IS UNITY WITH* J*ESUS, AND THE ASSURANCE OF* H*IS PROTECTION OVER YOU AND YOUR FAMILY EVEN IN THESE TROU-BLED TIMES.*

_____

_____

_____

_____

_____

_____

_____

_____

_____

_____

_____

_____

_____

_____

_____

_____

_____

_____

_____

_____

_____

_____

_____

_____

_____

_____

_____

_____

_____

_____

_____

_____

_____

WEEK 4

ARE YOU THE LIGHT OF THE WORLD?

-Exodus 34:29 (NIV) When Moses came down from Mount Sinai with the two tablets of the covenant law in his hands, he was not aware that his face was radiant because he had spoken with the LORD.

Wouldn't it be so AMAZING to have SUCH A CLOSE RELATIONSHIP WITH JESUS that we reflected HIS glory just as MOSES?

Well my friends, we can have that glory!

HOW?

The MORE we pursue the knowledge of Christ, remaining faithful to His teachings, listening to HIS voice, and OBEDIENT in the things He asks of us; we will elevate from glory to glory to glory.

The light within believers MANIFESTS outwardly--brighter and brighter.

This growth in Christ, developing a CLOSER relationship with HIM which increases the light; simultaneously extinguishes the darkness within us (our sinful nature from birth). IT'S A PROCESS.

> - Luke 11:36 (NLT) If you are filled with light, with
> no dark corners, then your whole life will be radiant,
> as though a floodlight were filling you with light."

Those who AREN'T seeking a relationship with Jesus and aren't interested whatsoever; don't UNDERSTAND this light of yours and may be resentful or AFRAID.

> -Exodus 34:30 (NLT) So when Aaron and the
> people of Israel saw the radiance of Moses' face, they
> were afraid to come near him.

Don't be discouraged; YOUR LIGHT is ATTRACTIVE to many who are hurting and suffering (due to life issues),your light is ATTRACTIVE to those who are experiencing an EMPTINESS in their lives (their hearts and souls) Your light is ATTRACTIVE to those who realize that something is missing and EVERYTHING they've tried to fill the void with isn't WORKING ; SO just know that JESUS lives in YOU and YOU are the light of the world– JESUS says so!!

> - Matthew 5:14 (NLT) "You are the light of the
> world—like a city on a hilltop that cannot be hidden.

My friends, know that you are on ASSIGNMENT to share the gospel and the light within you–--Jesus to this dark world.

> - John 1:5 (NLT) The light shines in the darkness,
> and the darkness can never extinguish it.

Our eyes of our hearts used to be covered with a veil, and we couldn't see nor understand THE TRUTH and the LOVE of JESUS our Lord & Savior–--nor did we reflect His glory.

- 2 Corinthians 3:14

... And this veil can be removed only by believing in Christ.

- 2 Corinthians 3:16 (NLT) But whenever someone turns to the Lord, the veil is taken away.

Believers are being CHANGED EVERYDAY to be MORE and MORE like JESUS.

MUSE

Day 1
Are You a Glorious Vessel?

Ephesians 5:8-9 says, *"For once you were full of darkness, but now you have light from the Lord. So live as people of light! For this light within you produces only what is good and right and true"* (NLT).

Everything of Jesus is pure and perfect—His character, His being. There's absolutely **no darkness** in Him—not a speck.

Mankind is naturally filled with darkness (a sinful nature) from birth. When a person chooses to live their life for Christ, a transformation begins and the heavenly brilliance of the Lord (who now dwells within) begins to cut through the darkness and change their way of thinking, view of life, and lifestyle.

In this process, the Lord displays who He is on earth **through** human vessels. As we learn more about Him and draw closer to Him, we become obedient to His commands (instructions) and our lives are enriched. Good things are being produced within us (His glorious character).

Good things such as:

✦ **Love**–loving **every** human being and certainly fellow believers.

✦ **Joy**- the joy that only comes from the Lord (a supernatural joy, not worldly happiness).

✦ **Peace**–a peace that only God can give, a peace that remains at **all times** during any crisis.

✦ **Patience, Kindness, Goodness, Faithfulness, Gentleness, and Self-control** (Galatians 5:22).

Each day, our character becomes more like the Lord Jesus. This **new** character becomes evident outwardly and produces good, godly deeds.

As this transformation continues, those around us are attracted to this beautiful glow and radiance from a glorious vessel filled with His light.

MUSE

DAY 2
IS THE FULLNESS OF GOD IN YOU?

C olossians 1:27 says, *"God's plan is to make known his secret to his people, this rich and glorious secret which he has for all peoples. And the secret is that Christ is in you, which means that you will share in the glory of God"* (GNT).

Jesus is the embodiment of the **fullness** of God (Colossians 2:9). All of the qualities and attributes of God are pure. They are so pure that mankind isn't worthy to be in the presence of the Savior of the world. However, He loves us so much and desires to be so close to us that when we surrender our hearts and invite Him in, He dwells within us forever. Jesus is the glory of God living in us.

The prophets of God and the people who obeyed God before Christ was born didn't understand the meaning of "the hope (assurance) of glory to come." It was a mystery to them. That "hope of glory" is Jesus. Those who **believe** in Him will share in this glory which is so rich; it will never run out.

The fullness of God in Christ is now in you.

MUSE

Day 3
Are You Producing Much Spiritual Fruit?

John 15:8 says, *"When you produce much fruit, you are my true disciples. This brings great glory to my Father"* (NLT).

The true glory of Jesus in you is transforming you and working through you producing fruit. Many of us enjoy fruit like apples, bananas, strawberries, and oranges. Fruit is healthy and good for you, supplying your body with natural nutrients.

The fruit being produced in your life by the spirit of the Lord, is a spiritual fruit which is equally beneficial for your **soul**.

"May you always be filled with the fruit of your salvation—the righteous character produced in your life by Jesus Christ—for this will bring much glory and praise to God." (Philippians 1:11 NLT).

Not only is this healthy for your character and your soul, but also for those around you. The new character being developed within, is appealing to others and beneficial to others. They will desire to live this fruitful life like yours, thus, drawing them to want to know more about the hope of glory within you. An apple tree doesn't consume its own apples; the apples are for the well-being of others.

As you remain connected to Jesus, you will produce more and more fruit and touch more of those around you bringing glory to God.

MUSE

Day 4
Are You Bringing
Glory to God?

1 Peter 2:12 says, *"Live such good lives among the pagans that, though they accuse you of doing wrong, they may see your good deeds and glorify God on the day he visits us"* (NIV).

Glory in, Glory out, Glory to God.

The glory within you is produced by the Spirit of the Lord Jesus. As you walk and grow in this new life in Christ, you're walking **through** this world, but your citizenship is in heaven, in the Kingdom of God. Believers are **only passing through**, headed to their ultimate and magnificent destination.

As we are walking through this world, it's imperative to know that the world is watching our conduct! So, we must behave ourselves in a manner that is pleasing to God and that glorifies God. We are AMBASSADORS of His kingdom.

The people of this world will mock you, criticize you, slander you, accuse you of doing wrong, persecute you, and will resent you because you do **not** partake of the sinful things they enjoy. Yes, some or all of these things will happen to you because you are a follower of Jesus and are of His kingdom which is **not** from this world.

When the nonbelievers of this world see your godly lifestyle and godly deeds, they will one day give glory to God.

Always remember, it is the Spirit of God who is "working in you both to will and to do for His good pleasure" (Philippians 2:13 NKJV), so make sure you give **all the glory to God.**

MUSE

DAY 5
ARE YOU GOD'S SHINING STAR?

Daniel 12:3 says, *"Those who are wise **will shine as bright as the sky**, and those who lead many to righteousness will **shine like the stars forever**"* (NLT).

This scripture is part of a passage of "End times" prophecy. The "end of days" will be the worst devastation that the world has ever experienced. Those who are wise are those who have come to repentance and have accepted Jesus as Lord.

Psalm 111:10 says, *"The fear of the Lord is the foundation of true wisdom. All who obey His commandments will grow in wisdom"* (NLT).

There will be many who are wise during the "End of days" during the great tribulation, the darkest times ever, and they will lead many to Christ and salvation. These Christians will shine like stars.

This is not just for the end times. There have been shining stars throughout the ages. Any believer who shares the gospel with others and lives a godly life, is a representative of the Kingdom of God and will lead or play a role in leading someone to Christ and salvation. The Christian is a light to lead those who are in spiritual darkness and headed for eternal condemnation, to salvation through the **Light** of the world, Jesus Christ, and to a more abundant life here on earth.

Most of the time, a believer will not know that their lifestyle and sharing the truth of Christ resulted in someone giving their life to Christ until they're in heaven.

These stars displaying God's glory will shine forever.

MUSE

Day 6
Are You Giving All Glory to God?

Isaiah 42:8 says, *"I am the LORD; that is my name! I will not give my glory to anyone else, nor share my praise with carved idols"* (NLT).

The nature of mankind, our sinful nature enjoys receiving recognition, praise for a job well done, accolades for accomplishments, and prestige for career positions and promotions. Even the most humble person desires some kind of glorification.

However, the Christian life is a life lived in service to our loving God and Savior. In this reborn life, the Christian becomes more like Christ (Romans 8:29). The believer begins to live life with more of a humble attitude and gratitude; understanding that anything good in us is from the transformative work of the Lord within us. Any of our good works and deeds are not of ourselves, but God working through us.

There's so much joy in serving the Lord, loving all people, and helping others. There will be times in which people will compliment your character, your accomplishments, and your deeds. You may receive praise and recognition, however, once the believer begins to keep the glory to him or herself, then pride creeps in. God hates pride. Pride is what led to Lucifer (satan) being cast out of heaven.

"Too much pride will destroy you" (Proverbs 16:18 CEV).

All glory belongs to God!

You can't prevent someone desiring to share their good feelings about you, but you (the believer) must be mindful and acknowledge that the glory belongs to God. The glory is not ours, although we are to reflect His glory, it **all** belongs to God, the source of all things.

DAY 7
MY JOURNAL

WRITE A LETTER OR PRAYER TO GOD THANKING HIM AND GIVING HIM ALL THE GLORY FOR ALL THAT HE HAS GIVEN YOU AND HELPED YOU TO ACCOMPLISH FOR HIM.

_____

_____

_____

_____

_____

_____

WEEK 5

ARE YOU A GOOD STEWARD OF GOD'S BLESSINGS?

We have an AWESOME GOD, He blesses each and every one of us. We will discover, if we think on a higher level, how the Lord Jesus has TRULY blessed us (not including our finances, we are SO blessed).

Many of us ONLY feel worthy in our society/culture, if we have a hefty bank account or an impressive stock/mutual fund portfolio.

We feel worthy if we can shop to the fullest desires of our hearts.

Many of us feel worthy if our home is the home of our dreams and filled with the furnishings of our hearts desires.

Many of us feel Worthy if we purchase the car we've ALWAYS WANTED.

MONEY is a RESOURCE Used to EXCHANGE for goods (your cash "goods" for NECESSITIES "goods" or DESIRES).

Your MONEY is a RESOURCE-- NOT the SOURCE!!

The AMOUNT of cash $ you have does NOT determine your IDENTITY.

Cash $$$$ does NOT increase your character (in a life-giving way) nor add to your integrity.

Your purchases / possessions: lavish home, designer clothing, jewelry fine art, and AMAZING vacations does NOT produce the person JESUS intends for you to be.

- Luke 12:15 (NLT) Then he said, "Beware! Guard against every kind of greed. Life is not measured by how much you own."

There's ABSOLUTELY NOTHING WRONG with having $$ WEALTH $$ and great things.

There is something wrong when your MONEY and your possessions HAVE YOU!

- Ecclesiastes 5:19 (NLT)

And it is a good thing to receive wealth from God and the good health to enjoy it. To enjoy your work and accept your lot in life—this is indeed a gift from God.

-Ecclesiastes 8:15 (NLT)

So I recommend having fun, because there is nothing better for people in this world than to eat, drink, and enjoy life. That way they will experience some happiness along with all the hard work God gives them under the sun.

God loves the rich and the poor EQUALLY:

- Proverbs 22:2

The rich and poor have this in common: The Lord made them both.

But, what defines a person is what they do with the God-given gifts, God-given talents, blessings- and CERTAINLY financial blessings.

Do we do good things with our MONEY which GOD has given us to assist others?

- 1 Timothy 6:18 (NLT) Tell them to use their money to do good. They should be rich in good works and generous to those in need, always being ready to share with others.

Are we ONLY doing the things which brings pleasure to self?

- Luke 12:17-19 (NLT)

17- He said to himself, 'What should I do? I don't have room for all my crops.'

-18 -Then he said, 'I know! I'll tear down my barns and build bigger ones. Then I'll have room enough to store all my wheat and other goods.

-19- And I'll sit back and say to myself, "My friend, you have enough stored away for years to come. Now take it easy! Eat, drink, and be merry!"'

Being blessed with abundance, especially financial abundance and not HAVING or WANTING a relationship with Jesus will end up disastrous for YOU:

- Luke 12:21 (NLT) "Yes, a person is a fool to store up earthly wealth but not have a rich relationship with God."

God has blessed you/us with all that we have, let's be a blessing to others:

- 2 Corinthians 9:8-9 (NLT) 8–And God will generously provide all you need. Then you will always have everything you need and plenty left over to share with others.

- 9 As the Scriptures say, "They share freely and give generously to the poor. Their good deeds will be remembered forever."

Many people have MONEY on their minds more than ANYTHING ELSE; MONEY is their priority- -
What happens when we "LOVE" money?

- Ecclesiastes 5:10 (NLT)

Those who love money will never have enough. How meaningless to think that wealth brings true happiness!

- 1 Timothy 6:10 (NLT) For the love of money is the root of all kinds of evil. And some people, craving money, have wandered from the true faith and pierced themselves with many sorrows.

- Hebrews 13:5 (NLT) Don't love money; be satisfied with what you have. For God has said, "I will never fail you. I will never abandon you."

Did you know that where you live, where you attend school, where you work, and EVERY SECOND of your LIFE has already been determined before you were born?

- Psalms 139:16 (NLT) You saw me before I was born. Every day of my life was recorded in your book. Every moment was laid out before a single day had passed.

Our Lord Jesus/ Almighty God has placed you / us right where we are in life and has blessed us with the gifts, talents, & finances to be a blessing to others.

- Deuteronomy 15:10 (NLT)

Give generously to the poor, not grudgingly, for the LORD your God will bless you in everything you do.

- Isaiah 32:8 (NLT)

But generous people plan to do what is generous, and they stand firm in their generosity.

Your God-given abilities & Talents are NOT ONLY for your benefit, but for the benefit of others.

Don't give because you're hoping the person gives back to you; give out of the goodness of your heart.

- Luke 6:32-34 (NLT) 32 "If you love only those who love you, why should you get credit for that? Even sinners love those who love them!

-33 And if you do good only to those who do good to you, why should you get credit? Even sinners do that much!

- 34 And if you lend money only to those who can repay you, why should you get credit? Even sinners will lend to other sinners for a full return.

For those who are stingy; a sobering message:

- Proverbs 11:24 (NLT) Give freely and become more wealthy; be stingy and lose everything.

- Proverbs 23:5 (NLT) In the blink of an eye wealth disappears, for it will sprout wings and fly away like an eagle.

Loving money $ may lead to foolishness
-Proverbs 21:20 (NLT)
The wise have wealth and luxury, but fools spend whatever they get.

RUMINATE

Day 1
Did You Know the Earth and everything in it Belongs to God?

Psalm 24:1, A psalm of David, says, *"The earth is the Lord's, and **everything** in it. The world and **all** its people belong to him"* (NLT emphasis added).

Planet Earth belongs to God and everything on and in it. Our bodies are precisely formed and shaped the way He intended (your height, weight, appearance, etc.).

God made you to perfection and He doesn't make mistakes. Our bodies belong to Him. Even the air we breathe is His air.

Mankind has been placed on earth to **manage** the things on earth. We don't own anything; we're simply stewards of them. Parents, your children are not yours. They are a gift from the Lord (Psalm 127:3 NLT). Parents are stewards, keepers of the gifts from the woman's womb, to raise them under God's Lordship for His purpose. Everything was made by God, for God, for His perfect reasons, even the things we can't see with the naked eye like molecules, atoms, etc.

Understanding that everything seen and unseen has been made strategically by the Lord Almighty, sets a clear perspective on the value we place on things. This should prompt all people to live life with a humble heart, realizing God's love and provision are for His prized possession—mankind.

However, we are quick to stake claim to some possession, causing us to love the material more than the Creator, a warped perspective. Having an abundance of things, goods, fame, position, and prestige should not be the focal point of life (although there's nothing wrong with these things). Almighty God is the focal point, the center of everything, and the source of all things because He created everything.

It all belongs to Him.

RUMINATE

Day 2
Did You Know God Sees Your Heart?

P salm 33:14-15 says, *"From his throne he observes all who live on the earth. He made their hearts, so he understands everything they do"* (NLT).

Our Heavenly Father, Creator of the universe, watches over **all** people intently. No one can escape the eyes of the Lord. He is completely focused. Not only does He microscopically observe every person's movement, but He knows our thoughts before we think them (Psalm 139:2 NLT).

He knows what we are going to say before we speak (Psalm 139:4 NKJV). Nothing in all of creation is hidden from our amazing Lord. It's wonderful that He watches us so closely and knows us so well. He observes and examines each of us with a fine-tooth comb, not to find the slightest fault, but because of His incomparable love for us.

In His intense observation of our comings, goings, and doings, many days, He protects us from external harm that we have no idea is headed our way. Quite often, He watches over us to protect us from ourselves in our willful sinful deeds. He cares for us, He wants to guide us in the right direction, and He desires an intimate relationship with us.

In His loving observation, He also sees the desires and motives of our hearts. He knows the deepest reasons for our desire to possess material things, for notoriety, fame, physical appearance improvement, position, power, and prestige.

The human heart is selfish, deceitful, and desperately wicked, and God searches all hearts and motives (Jeremiah 17:9-10 KJV).

God sees and knows all things.

RUMINATE

Day 3
Where Is Your Treasure?

M atthew 6:21 says, *"Wherever your treasure is, there the desires of your heart will also be"* (NLT).

Treasure is defined as wealth or riches stored or accumulated, especially in the form of precious metals, money, jewels. It is anything or a person greatly valued or highly prized.

There's absolutely nothing wrong with having nice things. If the Lord has showered His favor upon your life and has blessed you with riches, then by all means enjoy them with no regrets (Proverbs 10:22 CEV). However, the Lord isn't pleased if your possessions are in excess. This accumulation of goods has now become your treasure chest. The human heart can be easily steered towards the "beautiful things" the Lord has created. Thus, they become your first priority instead of the Lord having His rightful place in your heart as your priority.

The stock market investor closely keeps his or her eyes on the performance of their investment. Investing is perfectly okay unless the object of the investment has the investor's heart in knots or in bliss. **Where your treasure is, your heart will follow.**

The real estate mogul who SOLELY focuses on building his or her empire. **Where your treasure is, so is your heart.**

The fine arts collector who often gaze upon his/her collection. **Where your treasure is, your heart is sure to follow.**

When a person is a follower of our savior Jesus, that person desires to serve the Lord by loving all people, serving and helping others, being generous and giving. These are Kingdom commodities and are priceless and eternal. The Lord keeps a record of all these goods and the impact these goods have made in the lives of others. (Matthew 6:19-20 NLT). Your rewards may be realized here on earth, but MOST certainly, are waiting for you in heaven as well.

Your faith in Christ gives you the desire to obey His instructions. His Holy Spirit within you gives you the confidence to share the Good News about Jesus and the power to carry out the tasks He has set for you. At the same time, the Holy Spirit is transforming you to be more like Jesus resulting in His Kingdom being advanced here on earth and leading souls to Christ---SALVATION. The souls of people are precious treasures and are eternal. The material goods on earth cannot be taken to heaven and will remain on earth. Eventually, everything on earth will be destroyed including the earth itself.

Your treasure, your heart.

RUMINATE

Day 4
Do You Seek Worldly
Wisdom or Kingdom Wisdom?

Give and Take

Ecclesiastes 2:26 says, *"God gives wisdom, knowledge, and joy to those who please him. But if a sinner becomes wealthy, God takes the wealth away and gives it to those who please him. This, too, is meaningless—like chasing the wind"* (NLT).

Those who diligently seek the Lord, His written Word, His heart, His ways, His righteousness are wise. Kingdom wisdom is in stark contrast to worldly wisdom.

The wisdom of the world encourages a person to pursue and enhance **self**, "be all you can be", "the person who dies with the most toys wins", "get the best physique on the planet", wear the latest high-end apparel", "seek enormous wealth", "the world is mine", "always look out for number **one**."

The wisdom of the God of the Bible says, *"Do not love this world nor the things it offers you, for when you love the world, you do not have the love of the Father in you. For the world offers only a craving for physical pleasure, a craving for everything we see, and pride in our achievements and possessions. These are not from the Father, but are from this world*" (1 John 2:15-16 NLT).

The wisdom of God and His Kingdom says, "*Do not lean on your own understanding*" (Proverbs 3:5-6 NLT). "*Love God with all your heart and your neighbor as yourself*" (Luke 10:27 NLT). "*Don't repay evil with evil, but do good to all*" (1 Thessalonians 5:15 NLT). "*Help those in need*" (Psalm 112:9).

For the believer, Kingdom wisdom is exhibited in the usage of financial blessings from God, thus, bringing peace, joy, and a shower of blessings.

The Lord Jesus continues to **give** to those who trust in Him and do good.

At some point, God will **take** from the **non-believer** who has become rich and successful and or works day and night focusing on maintaining success, or striving to obtain more possessions, and will give it to those who have a heart to follow God's heart.

The success driven non-believer doesn't have a problem working 10, 12, or 14 hours a day to maintain or to reach a certain level of success. It's pure foolishness; it's **all** for self-gratification, self-glory, and self-indulgence based on **worldly wisdom.**

In their pursuit of wealth and self-glory, come sleepless nights, despair, along with days and nights without peace. Eventually, this person says, "Is this what life is all about? When I die, someone else is going to enjoy all that I've worked for my entire life? This is unfair! Life stinks!"

When you give of what the Lord has given to you, you will receive from God 30, 60, 100 times more than you have given.

RUMINATE

DAY 5
DO YOU TRUST IN WEALTH FOR SECURITY AND PROTECTION?

Proverbs 18:11 says, *"Rich people, however, imagine that their wealth protects them like high, strong walls around a city"* (GNT). Trusting in your money leads to the ruin of the soul.

In the days when Jesus walked the earth and hundreds of years before His birth, citizens of a city felt secure from outsiders and especially enemies by enclosing their city with high walls of huge stones. These stones were several feet in width, length, and height. These walls were built as a defense for the city and a deterrent to opposing nations. The city walls were intimidating. Its citizens and leaders strongly believed that **nothing** could breach these impenetrable walls or their safety.

Those who are wealthy feel the same. The rich feel so very secure in their wealth that they become prideful and arrogant. They trust in their wealth for the answer to everything. They don't see any need for God. Men and women of wealth believe that it's evidence of intelligence.

This wealth encourages one to become tight-fisted; not realizing that the Lord gave them their success (Deuteronomy 8:18 NLT) and they become increasingly unwilling to generously help those in need because it may poke a hole in their **"great wall"** of financial security.

This "financial wall of defense" is no match for **death**, some sort of **debilitating disease**, and eternal condemnation.

Trusting in your money as security is placing this resource above all else; becoming an idol (Leviticus 19:4 NLT), a god in your heart.

The Lord God is our defense, security, and refuge (Proverbs 18:10 NLT). He is who we trust in, He is who we run to for safety, security, and protection.

Trust in your money and down you go (Proverbs 11:28 NLT).

RUMINATE

DAY 6
WHAT IS YOUR HEART
TETHERED TO?

Malachi 3:10 says, *"Bring all the tithes into the storehouse so there will be enough food in my Temple. If you do,"* says the LORD *of Heaven's Armies, "I will open the windows of heaven for you. I will pour out a blessing so great you won't have enough room to take it in! Try it! Put me to the test!"* (NLT).

Tithe is a Hebrew term which means tenth. When believers give tithes and offerings, it's one of many ways in which we honor and worship our Lord God.

In antiquity, "storehouse" refers to a special room in the temple to store tithed items. God says to bring **all** the tithes into the storehouse. Yes, tithe is a tenth of your earnings. In the New Testament, the Apostle Paul tells the church and the reader to give whatever amount the Lord has placed on your heart as an offering which is anything above your regular tithe.

When we honor the Lord with our tithes and offerings, He **promises** to bless us beyond our wildest imagination. It's important to know that **everything** we have comes from Him, especially our earnings. So, when we give our tithe, we are giving back to God a tiny percentage of what He has given to us.

When we worship the Lord in tithes and offerings, He uses it and multiplies it to bless those in need. The Lord can use $1, multiply it, and spread it out 4,000 ways or more. Jesus fed 5,000 in Mark 6:41-43.

Our Heavenly Father is to never be put to a test, however, in this scripture it is the only place in the entire Bible where He asks to be tested in His promise to pour out blessings so great, you can't contain it—if His people (believers) will give and tithe. Why? Because the Lord knows that the human heart is tethered to his/her wallet.

Picture tithing and offering like playing catch with God. You toss God a golf ball, He catches it and tosses back to you a softball. You toss Him the softball, He catches it, and tosses back to you a basketball. You toss Him the basketball, and He tosses back to you a beach ball.

This is what tithing is like and we can never out give God. The more we give to Him, the **greater** He gives to us. We must know, that our giving and tithing **has to** be from a sincere heart. We are not to give so that we may receive.

God loves to bless His children and He desires for us to have a heart like His, to be a blessing to others. When we give from a sincere heart, He blesses us with an amazing, unexplainable joy, and HE also PROMISES to take care of ALL of OUR NEEDS. (2 Corinthians 9:7-9 NASB) Over time, cheerful giving will become a lifestyle.

My heart, my tithe.

DAY 7
MY JOURNAL

WRITE A LETTER OR PRAYER TO GOD THANKING HIM FOR THE BLESSINGS OF AN ABUNDANT LIFE.

_____

_____

_____

_____

_____

_____

_____

_____

_____

_____

_____

_____

_____

_____

_____

_____

_____

_____

_____

_____

_____

_____

_____

_____

_____

INVITATION

If you have not accepted Jesus as your Lord and savior, I want to encourage you to make this decision, right now, in this moment.

This will be the best decision you will ever make.

Just repeat this short prayer out loud. You can do this privately, in your closet, in your car, wherever you choose.

"Lord Jesus, I know that I am a sinner and that I need You. Please forgive me for all I have done wrong. Please come into my life and begin to lead me. I pray this as sincerely as I know how. Amen."

If you repeated this prayer and meant it from the bottom of your heart, you are instantly a child of God.

Heaven and eternal life are yours and it's guaranteed!

A NOTE FROM THE AUTHOR

For many years, my all-time favorite movie was "Wall Street." There's a famous line in the movie where the star says, "Greed is good." I truly believed that "greed was good" and applied that to my life. I lived it, I loved it.

The things of this world are temporal; the soul of a man is eternal. Our investment, while on this earth, should be in the things of the kingdom of God which are eternal.

The road to eternal destruction is broad, and many travel it, but the road to eternal life is narrow and few find it. Allow the wisdom of the spirit of the Lord to guide you down the road of right living; there will be difficulties, but the grace of the Lord is rewarding and all you need.

Choosing Jesus as the Lord of my life is the best choice I ever made, and I'm certain it'll be the best decision you will ever make. I still have a long way to go, but my faith is in Him alone. I pray you have made that choice now as well. – Dervon Dunagan

A Final thought for you...

ABOUT THE AUTHOR

B orn in 1965, raised in Pasadena, California. I'm a husband to an amazing wife of 32 years, and a father to four incredible children; three sons and one daughter–all adults. I'm also an elated grandparent of two.

I'm a proud employee of the United States Postal Service for 35 years and still going strong, but the finish line is very near.

At the age of 14, in 1979, I accepted Jesus as my Lord and savior, however all of my teenage years and most of my adult years, my life was anything BUT Christ like. As a husband and father, I learned so much about life, and about myself. Along the way, I made MANY mistakes as a husband and father which I deeply regret.

I experienced trials, triumphs, setbacks, and heartaches, but what I didn't realize, God was doing a work in me. In all of my endeavors: licensed real estate agent, loan agent, stock market investments, multiple rental properties, and an assistant coach for youth sports, there was a craving that I couldn't satisfy. There was something missing, a void, emptiness that I couldn't fill.

In 2010, I recommitted my life to Christ full throttle; Jesus filled that void, that emptiness. I dove head first into God's word (the Bible) daily, listening to Christian radio sermons to and from work, hosting small group Bible study weekly, attending and graduating the school of ministry in 2017, and partnering with a dear friend to launch a men's ZOOM bible study in the midst of the 2020 Coronavirus pandemic.

The insatiable desire for the things of this world and all it offered; God used that burning desire and transformed it into a HUNGER to know Him and please Him.

This hunger within me is none other than the holy spirit of the Lord, passionately guiding me to author this book.

All the thanks and glory to God, for the trials, travails, and triumphs in my life. I'm still a work in progress, God is not finished with me. I'm NOT where I wanna be, but I'm not where I USED to be.

I praise the Lord for the peaks and valleys of life; life is a journey and each day is a journey WITHIN the journey.

Each day has meaning and purpose, so the Lord has placed in my heart this yearning to share the good news about Him to every soul that He brings into my life--extended family, friends, colleagues, and neighbors.

My prayer for you, is that you will experience your journey with Christ, and receive all of the joy and fulfillment it will bring.

May God richly bless you in all that you do

Dervon Dunagan

Contact info: https://m.facebook.com/
Answers-4-Life-1047415948691514/

Keep in touch with this link for future books by Dervon.